It's Hanukkah!

by Richard Sebra

BUMBA BOOKS™

LERNER PUBLICATIONS ◆ MINNEAPOLIS

Note to Educators:

Throughout this book, you'll find critical thinking questions. These can be used to engage young readers in thinking critically about the topic and in using the text and photos to do so.

Lerner Publications Company
A division of Lerner Publishing Group, Inc.
241 First Avenue North
Minneapolis, MN 55401 USA

For reading levels and more information, look up this title at www.lernerbooks.com.

Library of Congress Cataloging-in-Publication Data

Names: Sebra, Richard, 1984– author.
Title: It's Hanukkah! / by Richard Sebra.
Description: Minneapolis, MN : Lerner Publications, [2016] | ©2016 | Series: Bumba books—It's a Holiday! | Includes index. | "K to grade 3, ages 4–8"—ECIP data view.
Identifiers: LCCN 2016003155 (print) | LCCN 2016003679 (ebook) | ISBN 9781512414271 (lb : alk. paper) | ISBN 9781512414974 (pb : alk. paper) | ISBN 9781512414981 (eb pdf)
Subjects: LCSH: Hanukkah—Juvenile literature.
Classification: LCC BM695.H3 S3934 2016 (print) | LCC BM695.H3 (ebook) | DDC 296.4/35—dc23

LC record available at http://lccn.loc.gov/2016003155

Manufactured in the United States of America
1 – VP – 7/15/16

LERNER
SOURCE

Expand learning beyond the printed book. Download free, complementary educational resources for this book from our website, www.lerneresource.com.

Table of Contents

We Celebrate Hanukkah

Hanukkah is a Jewish holiday.

It lasts eight days.

It happens in November or December.

Hanukkah is an old holiday.

It began thousands of years ago.

It celebrated the opening of

a temple.

Hanukkah is called the Festival

of Lights.

People put candles in a holder.

Why might Hanukkah be called the Festival of Lights?

There are nine candles.

The middle candle is used

to light the others.

A new candle is lit each

night.

Why do you think there are nine candles?

People sing songs.

They sing after the candles are lit.

Some songs are about lights.

Others are about games.

Why do you think people sing songs?

13

Children play games during Hanukkah.

They spin a top.

The top has four sides.

Why might the top have writing on it?

Families eat meals together.

Many families eat fried foods.

They also eat foods made

with cheese.

Children get gifts.

The gifts may be coins.

The gifts may be candy.

The gifts may be toys.

Hanukkah is a great holiday.

Families celebrate it together.

Candles at Hanukkah

The candles go in the holder.
Put them in from right to left.
Use the middle candle to light the others.
Light the candles from left to right.

Picture Glossary

candles

wax sticks that can be burned for light

celebrate

to do something fun on a special day

temple

a place where people pray

top

a small toy that spins

Index

Read More

Felix, Rebecca. *We Celebrate Hanukkah in Winter.* Ann Arbor, MI: Cherry Lake Publishing, 2014.

Pettiford, Rebecca. *Hanukkah.* Minneapolis: Jump!, 2014.

Strain Trueit, Trudi. *Hanukkah.* Mankato, MN: The Child's World, 2013.

Photo Credits